LUQMAN'S ADVICE TO HIS SON

Quran Stories for Little Hearts

by

S Khan

Goodwordkidz
Helping you build a family of faith

Long long ago, there lived a wise man whose name was Luqman. He was probably the grandson of a sister or an aunt of the Prophet Ayyub (Job) ﷺ.

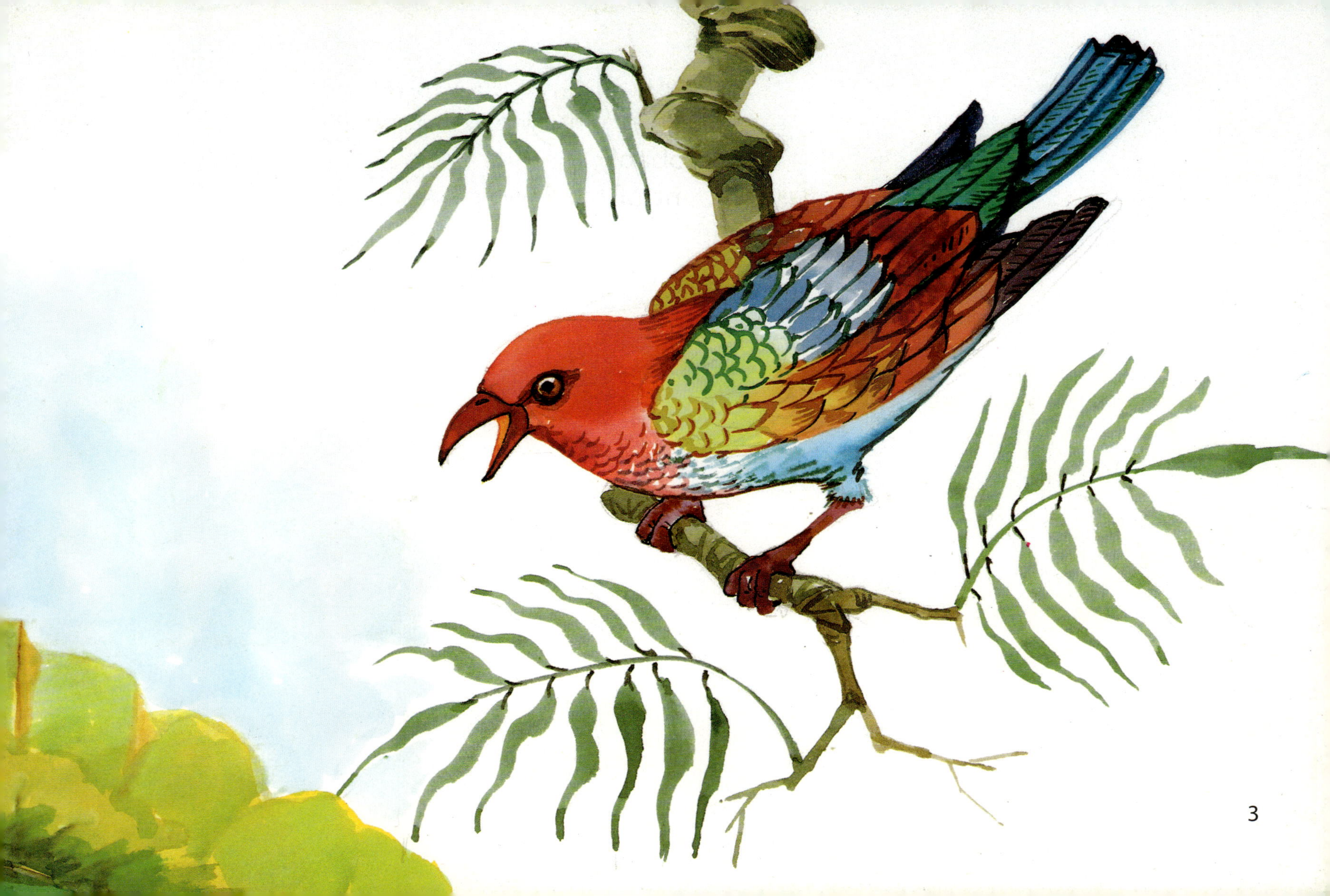

Allah gave him wisdom and asked him to be thankful to the Almightly, saying: "He that gives thanks to Allah has much to gain, but if anyone denies Allah's favours, then Allah is self-sufficient and glorious."

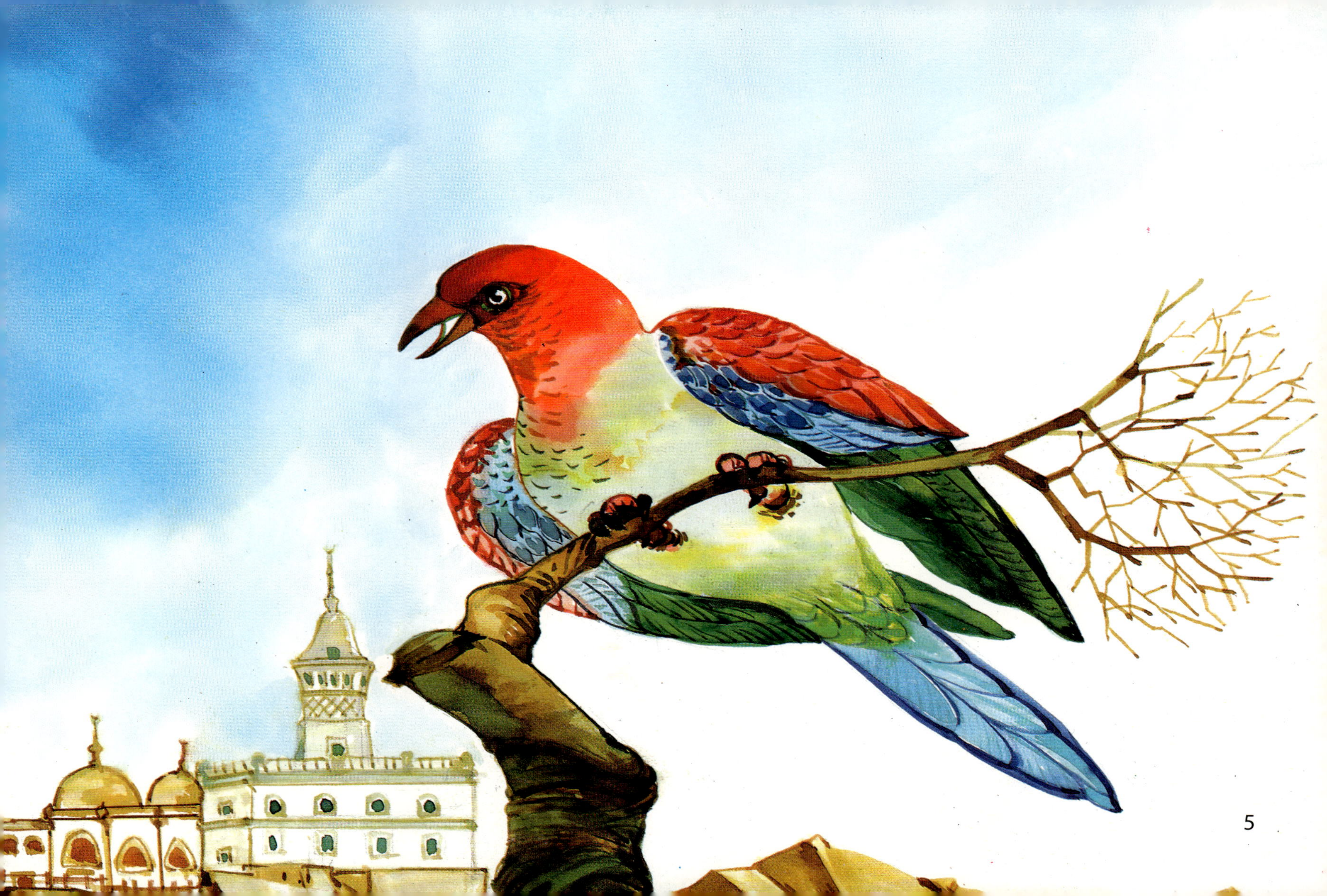

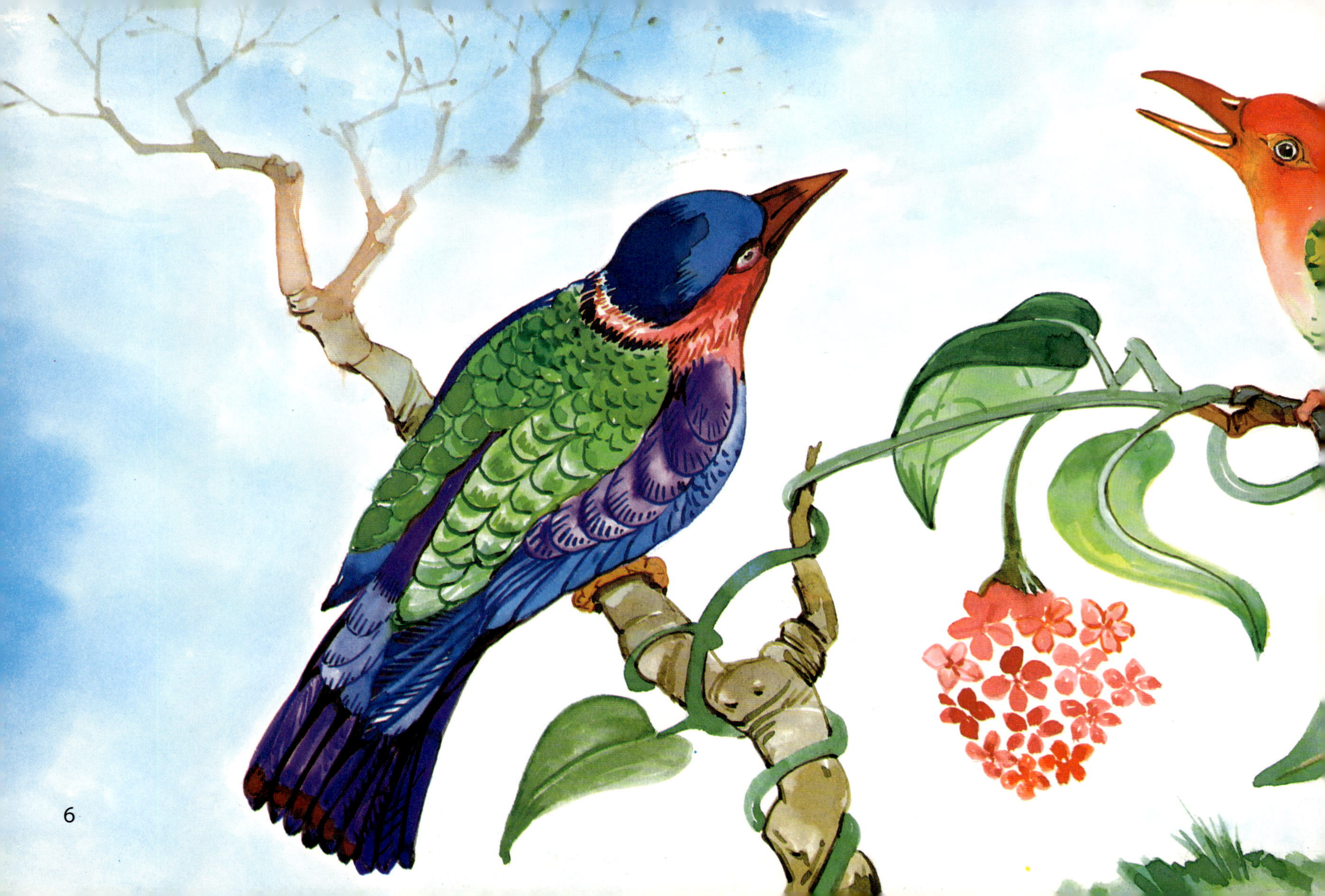

One day Luqman called his son and gave him some wise counsel. He said, "O my little son, serve no other deity besides Allah; for idolatry is an abominable sin."

Luqman said, "My son, Allah will bring all things to light, be they small as a grain of mustard seed, be they hidden inside a rock or in heaven or earth. Gracious is Allah and all-knowing."

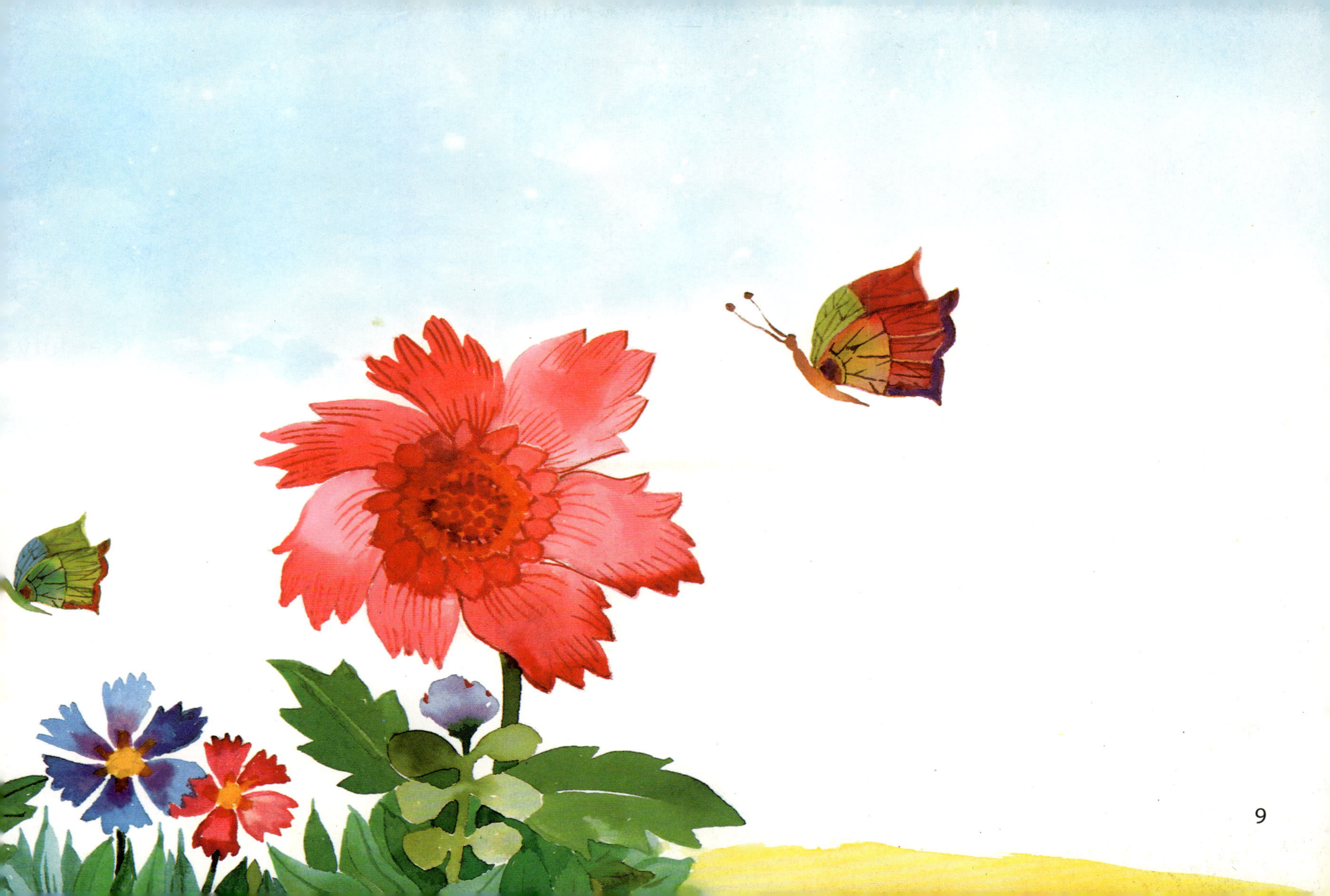

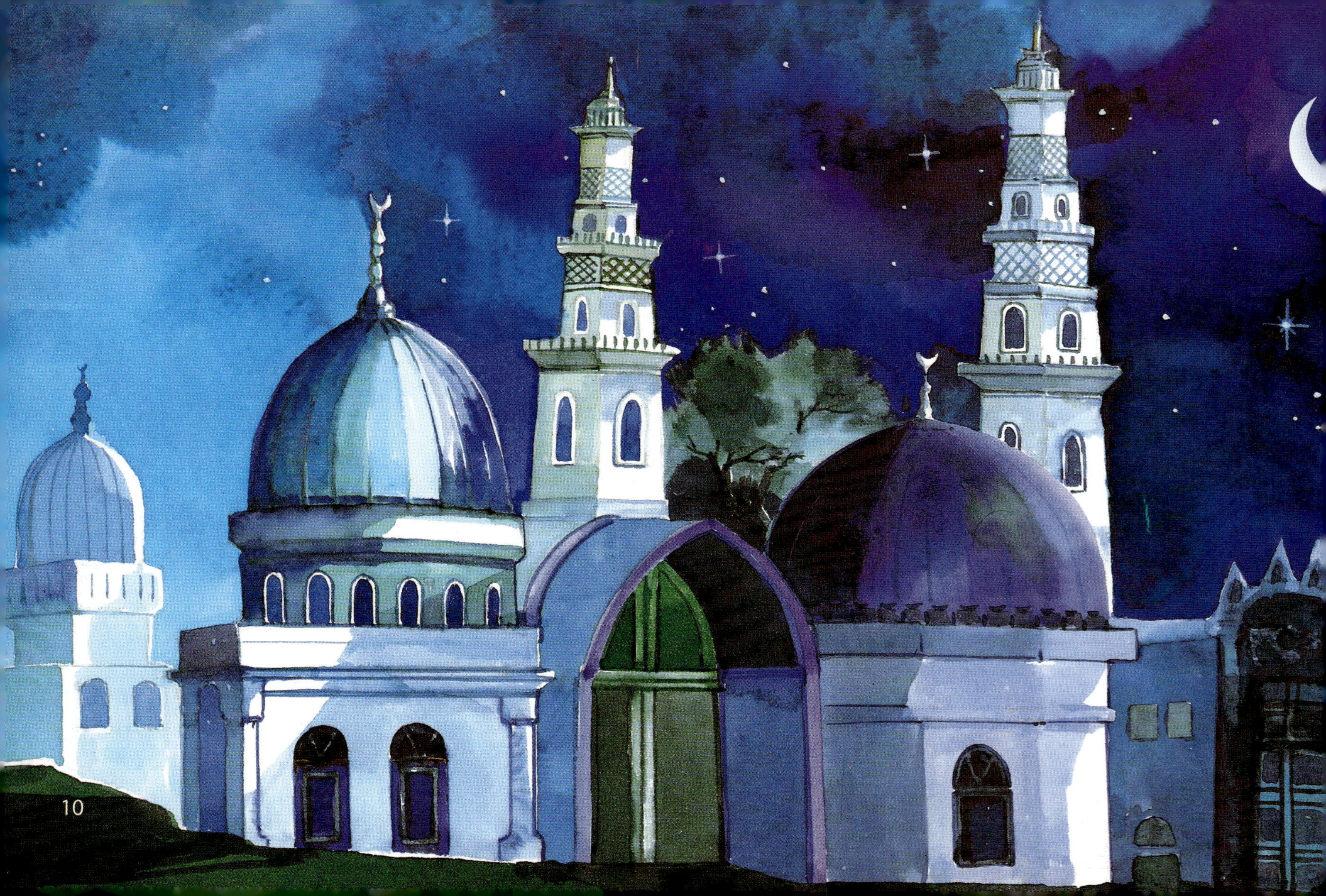

Luqman continued, "My son, be regular in prayer."

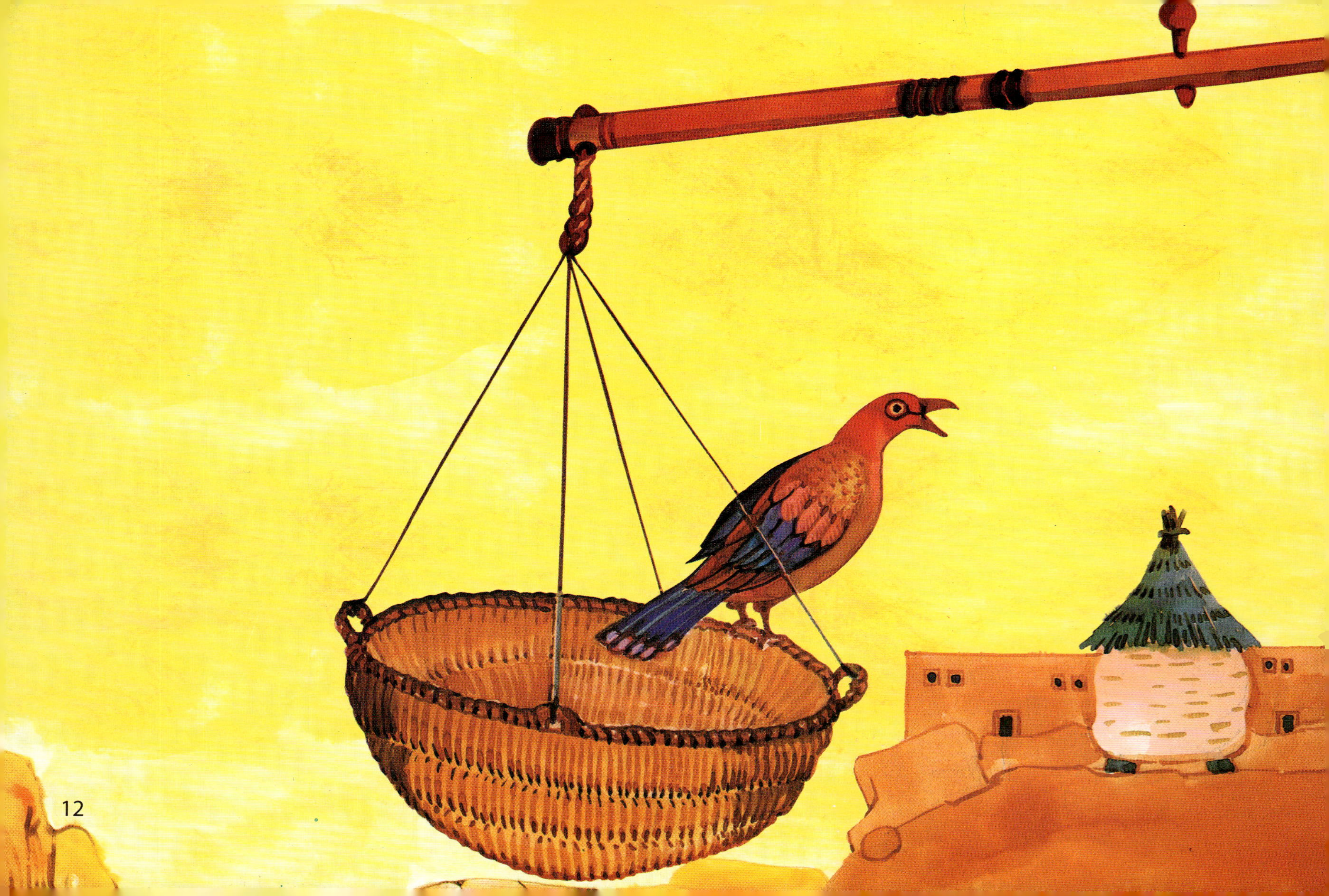

Luqman also advised him to speak out for justice and forbid evil.

14

"Put up patiently with whatever happens to you", continued Luqman, "that is a duty for all."

Luqman further advised his son: "Do not treat men with scorn."

17

Luqman also told his son: "Do not walk proudly on the earth."

19

"God does not love the arrogant and the boastful." said Luqman.
"Rather let your walk be modest."

21

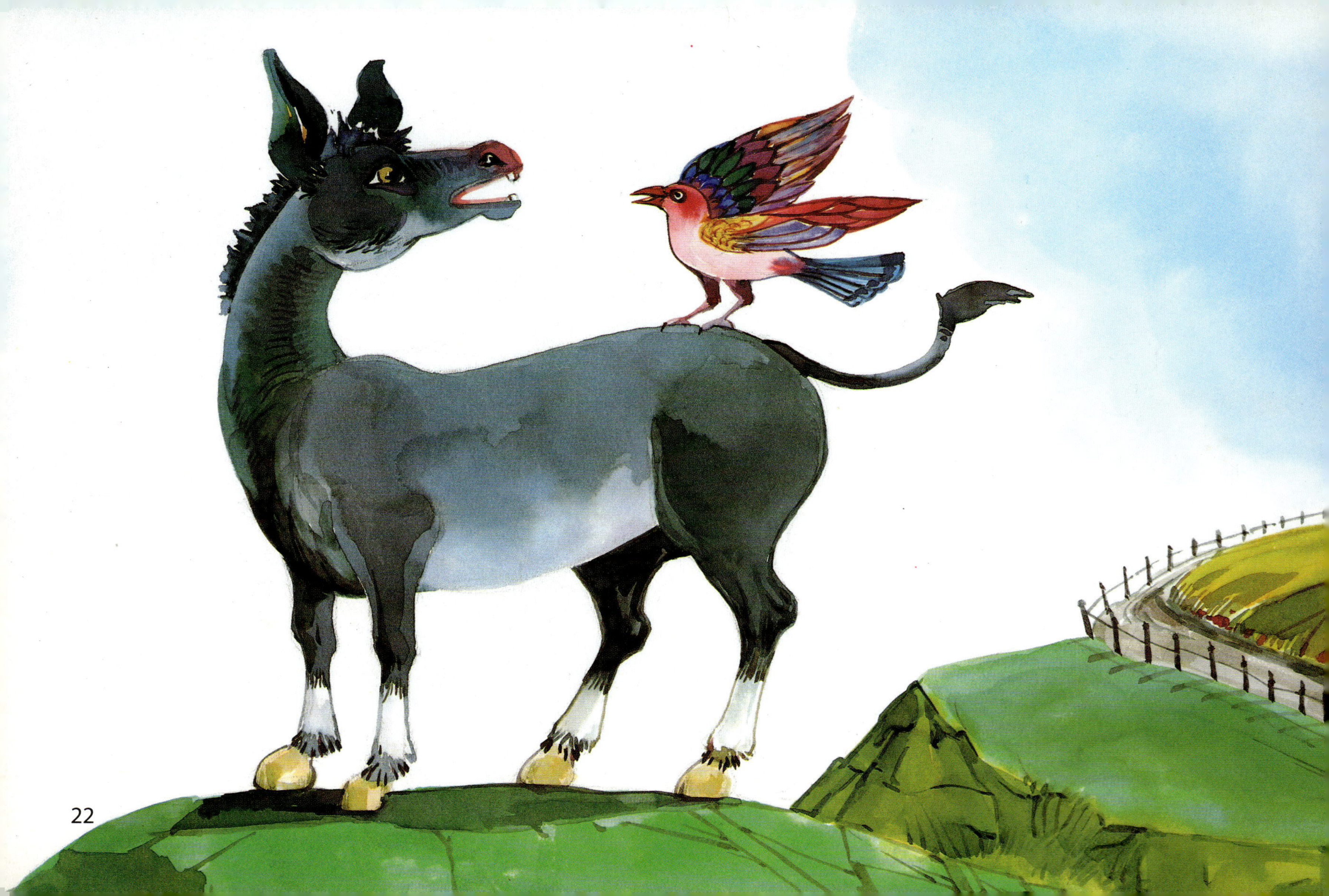

The last advice which Luqman gave to his son was to be polite: "Keep your voice low. The harshest of voices is the braying of the ass."

Luqman's wise advice to his son is for all of us to follow so that we may become good human beings.

Find Out More
To know more about the message and meaning of Allah's words, look up the following parts of the Quran which tell the story of Luqman.
Surah Luqman 31:12